10/12

The U.S. Supreme Court

by Anastasia Suen

illustrated by Matthew Skeens

EQUAL JUSTICE UNDER L

PICTURE WINDOW BOOKS
Minneapolis, Minnesota

Special thanks to our advisers for their expertise:

Kevin Byrne, Ph.D., Professor of History
Gustavus Adolphus College, St. Peter, Minnesota

Terry Flaherty, Ph.D., Professor of English
Minnesota State University, Mankato

Editor: Jill Kalz
Designer: Abbey Fitzgerald
Page Production: Melissa Kes
Art Director: Nathan Gassman
Associate Managing Editor: Christianne Jones
The illustrations in this book were created digitally.
Photo Credit: Shutterstock/pxlar8, 23

Picture Window Books
151 Good Counsel Drive, P.O. Box 669
Mankato, MN 56002-0669
877-845-8392
www.picturewindowbooks.com

Library of Congress Cataloging-in-Publication Data
Suen, Anastasia.
The U.S. Supreme Court / by Anastasia Suen ; illustrated by Matthew Skeens.
p. cm. — (American symbols)
Includes index.
ISBN 978-1-4048-4707-1 (library binding)
1. United States. Supreme Court—History—Juvenile literature. 2. Judicial power—
United States—Juvenile literature. I. Skeens, Matthew. II. Title.
KF8742.S84 2008
347.73'26—dc22   2008006346

Table of Contents

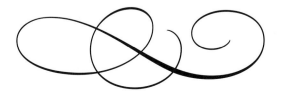

My name is Marta. I'm a lawyer. I've come to the U.S. Supreme Court to talk about my case. The Supreme Court is the highest court in the United States. Its building is a symbol of the country's highest law.

Nine Judges

Today's U.S. Supreme Court is made up of nine judges, called justices. The justices' job is to make sure the words of the U.S. Constitution are followed. One justice is the chief justice.

EQUAL JUSTICE UNDER LAW

Supreme Court justices are picked by the president and approved by the Senate (a part of Congress). They serve until they retire, quit, are asked to leave, or die.

The Judicial Branch

The U.S. government is divided into three parts, or branches—Judicial, Legislative, and Executive. The Judicial Branch is the court system. It makes sure that laws are carried out in the right way. The Supreme Court is part of the Judicial Branch.

Each branch of the U.S. government has different powers. But no one branch is stronger than the others. Each branch is equal.

Capitol

LEGISLATIVE

White House

EXECUTIVE

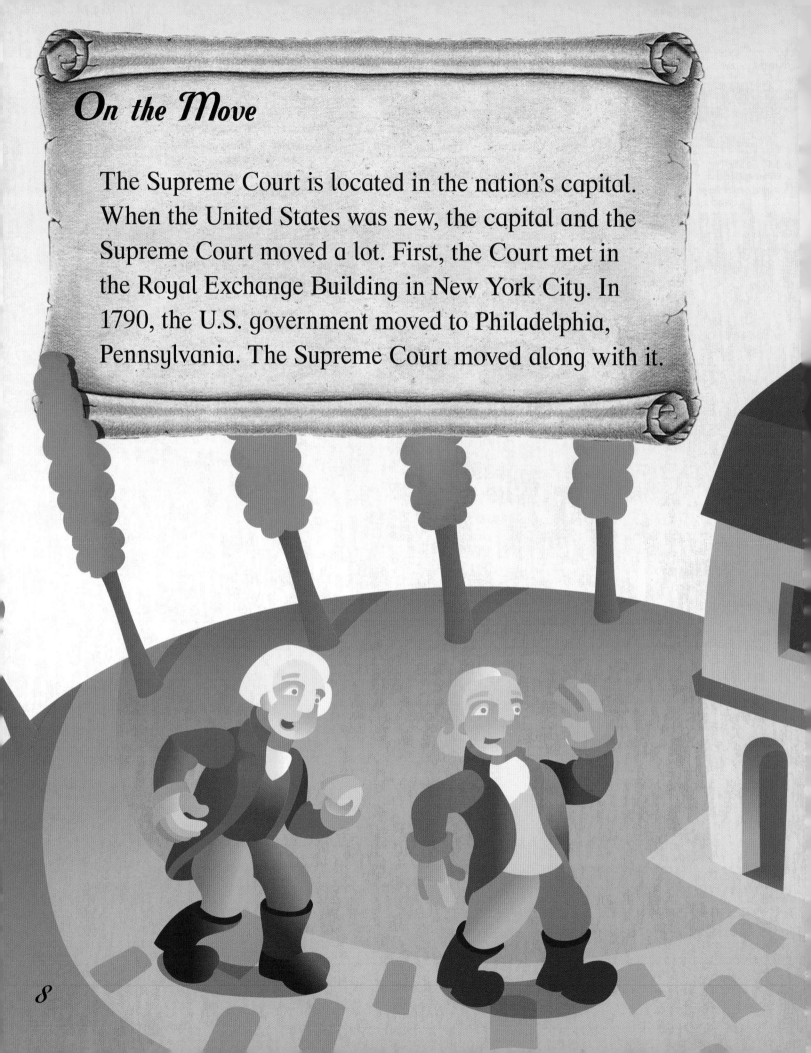

On the Move

The Supreme Court is located in the nation's capital. When the United States was new, the capital and the Supreme Court moved a lot. First, the Court met in the Royal Exchange Building in New York City. In 1790, the U.S. government moved to Philadelphia, Pennsylvania. The Supreme Court moved along with it.

Royal Exchange Building

While in Philadelphia, the U.S. Supreme Court met in two different buildings—Independence Hall and then City Hall.

Sharing a Building

In 1800, the U.S. government moved to Washington, D.C. The Supreme Court followed. It shared the Capitol building with Congress, using a number of different rooms. From 1860 to 1935, the Court met in the Old Senate Chamber.

After the British set fire to the U.S. Capitol during the War of 1812, the Supreme Court met in a private house for a short time.

A Home of Its Own

In 1929, Chief Justice William Howard Taft wanted the Supreme Court to have a home of its own. Congress agreed. Soon plans for the Supreme Court Building began to take shape. Work began in 1932.

Taft held two top jobs in the United States. He was president from 1909 to 1913. He later became chief justice of the Supreme Court.

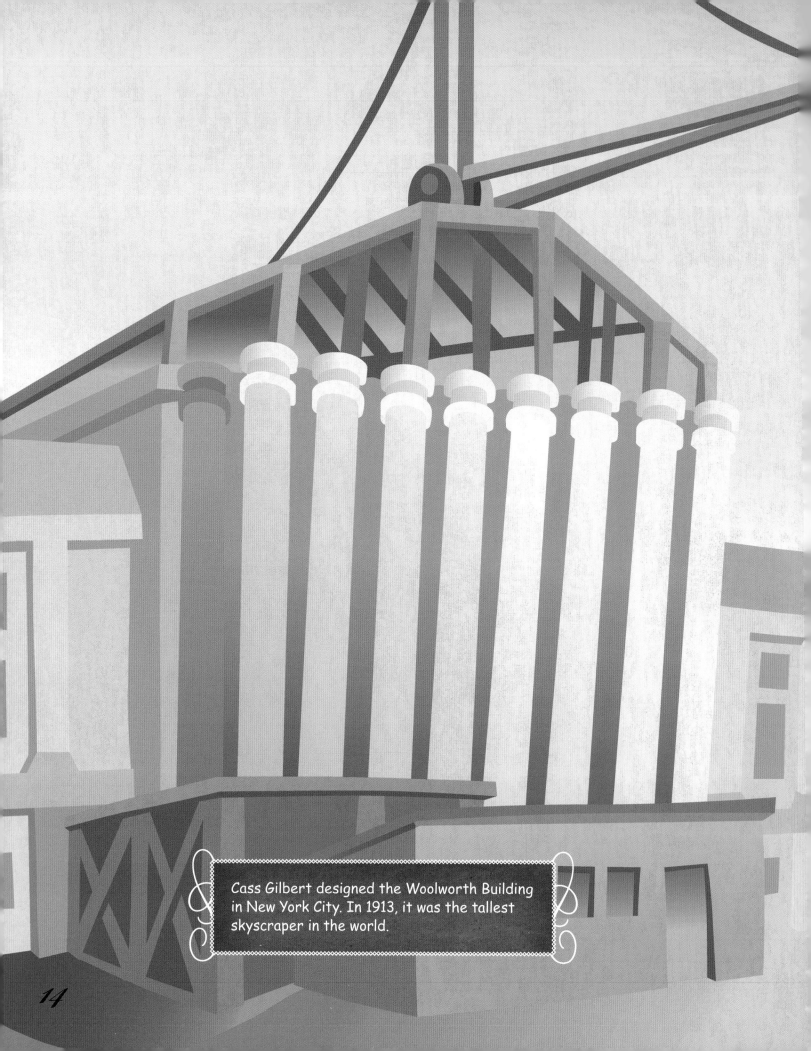

Cass Gilbert designed the Woolworth Building in New York City. In 1913, it was the tallest skyscraper in the world.

An Architect

Taft asked Cass Gilbert to design the U.S. Supreme Court Building. Gilbert had designed the capitols for Minnesota, West Virginia, and Arkansas. He also designed other famous buildings. Gilbert designed the Supreme Court Building to match other buildings in the capital city.

The Supreme Court Building

Three years later, in 1935, the U.S. Supreme Court Building was completed.

Almost square, the building measures 385 feet (117 meters) from front to back and 304 feet (93 m) from side to side. Its walls, floors, columns, and sculptures are made of marble from all around the world.

UNDER LAW

Sixteen columns stand at the main entrance to the U.S. Supreme Court Building. Above the columns are the words *Equal Justice Under Law*.

A Look Inside

Just inside the main entrance lies the Great Hall. Marble columns and busts of former chief justices line the walls.

18

Offices fill most of the Supreme Court Building's main floor and second floor. The third floor is the Supreme Court Library. It holds more than 500,000 law books. Justices and staff members use these books for research.

The bronze doors at the main entrance to the U.S. Supreme Court Building weigh 6.5 tons (6 metric tons) each. They don't swing out when they open. They slide into the wall.

The Court Chamber

The Supreme Court meets to hear cases in the Court Chamber. Seats in the chamber are painted red or black. The red benches on the left are for the media. The red benches on the right are for guests. The black chairs in front of the benches are for officers of the Court and important visitors.

About 8,000 cases are submitted to the U.S. Supreme Court each year. Only about 100 to 150 are heard.

The U.S. Supreme Court justices hear cases from October to May. They discuss the facts with one another and then make a decision. Once the Court's decision is read, it cannot be changed.

Maybe one day you can work inside this important American symbol as a lawyer or judge!

U.S. Supreme Court Facts

U.S. Supreme Court Building

- President George Washington picked John Jay (1745–1829) to be the first chief justice of the U.S. Supreme Court.

- Because there is an uneven number of justices on the U.S. Supreme Court, there can never be a tie.

- The outside walls of the U.S. Supreme Court Building are made of marble from Vermont. It took 1,000 freight train cars to carry the stone to Washington, D.C.

- In 2003, work began to make the Supreme Court Building bigger. A two-story underground addition was built for the Court Police. The Court Police keep everyone in the building safe.

- The Supreme Court Building has more than 1 million visitors each year. Its cafeteria is open to the public and is known for its good food and fair prices.

Glossary

architect — a person who designs buildings

bust — a sculpture of a person's head and shoulders

case — a set of facts

Congress — the group of people in the U.S. government that make laws

court — a place where laws are carried out; also, a gathering headed by a judge or judges

symbol — an object that stands for something else

U.S. Constitution — the plan for how the U.S. government works

War of 1812 — (1812–1815) the war between the United States and Great Britain over unfair British control of shipping; often called the "Second War of Independence"

To Learn More

More Books to Read

Elish, Dan. *The U.S. Supreme Court*. New York: Children's Press, 2007.

Harris, Nancy. *What's the Supreme Court?* Chicago: Heinemann Library, 2008.

Hempstead, Anne. *The Supreme Court*. Chicago: Heinemann Library, 2006.

Taylor-Butler, Christine. *The Supreme Court*. New York: Children's Press, 2008.

On the Web

FactHound offers a safe, fun way to find Web sites related to topics in this book. All of the sites on FactHound have been researched by our staff.

1. Visit *www.facthound.com*

2. Type in this special code: 1404847073

3. Click on the FETCH IT button.

Your trusty FactHound will fetch the best sites for you!

Index

Look for all of the books in the American Symbols series:

Angel Island

The Bald Eagle

The Bill of Rights

Ellis Island

The Great Seal of the United States

The Liberty Bell

The Lincoln Memorial

Our American Flag

Our National Anthem

Our U.S. Capitol

The Pledge of Allegiance

The Statue of Liberty

Uncle Sam

The U.S. Constitution

The U.S. Supreme Court

The White House